SCRAWNY TO BRAWNY IN 8 WEEKS

BY

PAUL NAM

For more works by this author, please visit:

www.pursefitness.com

www.theworkoutloft.com

https://payhip.com/wy2kool

OTHER BOOKS BY THE AUTHOR

FIT TO FAT IN 8 WEEKS

SCRAWNY TO BRAWNY IN 8 WEEKS

NUTRITION 101: BUILDING THE FOUNDATION

IMMUNE SYSTEM 8: BOOST YOUR IMMUNE SYSTEM NATURALLY

IT'S ALL ABOUT YOUR HEALTH: FOOD RECIPES

THE BOOK OF CHOICES: THE LIVES OF 2 ATHLETES

BODYBUILDING AND STEROIDS: MY PERSONAL STORY

DUMBBELL TRAINING: FOR MEN AND WOMEN

DUMBBELL AND CORE(ABS) TRAINING: FOR MEN AND WOMEN

LEARN HOW TO STRETCH: FOR BETTER MOVEMENT AND HEALTH

BEGINNER'S GUIDE TO DIET AND TRAINING

TABLE OF CONTENTS

INTRODUCTION

It all starts with a vision.

What is your vision? Some dream to be financially rich while others want to travel around the world. When we are young we often try to find an identity that will suit us. Some grow up to be doctors, firefighters, business owners, and a few even become famous actors.

Along that journey most people encounter some form of training, whether it be martial arts, boxing, yoga, or even weight training. Those who fall in love with weight training become gym rats and often try to create a lifestyle around it.

The lifestyle of a hardcore bodybuilder or fitness model is nothing but glamorous. Sure they look amazing but they eat copious amounts of food, train all the time, and most use performance enhancing drugs. Yet millions of people around the world are addicted to the lifestyle.

Creating a physique is serious work. You have to train hard in the gym, constantly eat to feed your muscles, and get the needed rest to help with muscle growth.

But the rewards are worth it, the way people look at you at the beach, the gym, and in the general public.

Welcome to Scrawny to Brawny in 8 Weeks. This book will help you gain some serious muscle if you follow these guidelines.

Remember to train hard, but smart!

THE MAJOR NUTRIENTS

If you have read my Fat To Fit book, you can skip this chapter and the next or read it again.

No training book is complete about learning the basics. Just like learning how to walk or ride a bike, there is a process.

In order to grow, you need to feed your body constantly. This requires the proper nutrients at all times. The basic nutrients are what you feed your body daily. The basics are water, protein, carbohydrates, fats, vitamins, and minerals.

This chapter will teach you briefly about the different classes of nutrients.

PROTEINS

Protein is found in many foods, such as meats, legumes, and some cereal products. The proteins that are in your body have many roles, including being an energy source. They are also a major structural material in many parts of your body, such as muscle, bone, and skin. Proteins allow us to move, works with the immune system to keep us healthy, and regulates many chemical reactions needed for life.

The best sources are steak, chicken, whole eggs, turkey, fish, pork, beans, protein powder, dairy products, and lean ground meats.

If you're vegan, choose tofu, seeds, quinoa, beans, and non-dairy protein powders.

CARBOHYDRATES

There are many different types of carbohydrates as those found in foods like rice and pasta, verses foods like fruits and desserts. The most important carbohydrate is glucose because our cells use glucose as their primary source of energy. Other than tasting good, carbohydrates are used for other purposes as well. Some are needed to make the DNA that is inside of your cells. Certain carbohydrates like dietary fiber help to maintain the health of your digestive system. Like proteins, carbohydrates are also important structural components in the membranes that surround the cells in your body.

The best sources of carbohydrates should come from whole grains, fruits, and vegetables. Man-made carbohydrates, like pasta, should be secondary and it's best to limit or eliminate refined sugars, such as candy.

Now onto the next, fats.

FATS

Fats are found in a variety of oils, foods, and in the human body. They provide energy to the body, are important for the structure of cell membranes, and are needed for the development of your nervous and reproductive system.

Just remember one rule, eat more omega 3 than omega 6 fatty acids.

The best sources of fats come from fatty fish, omega3, flaxseed oil, nuts, seeds, extra virgin olive oil, avocados, and cheese.

WATER

Water makes up about 60% of your total body weight so it is important to stay hydrated. The functions are very important as it helps to transport nutrients, gases, and waste products. Water also helps to regulate your body temperature and protects your internal organs from damage.

The suggested guideline for water intake for adult females is 10-11cups of water daily from both drinks and food. Men should have 13-14 cups of water from drinks and food.

VITAMINS

Vitamins are found in most foods but are abundant in fruits, vegetables, and grains. Your body needs vitamins to regulate chemical reactions and to promote growth and development.

Some vitamins are called antioxidants, which help to protect your body from toxic compounds such as air pollution.

Vitamins are classified as either water or fat soluble. The fat soluble vitamins are A,D,E,K, and the water soluble vitamins are B, and C.

The best sources for vitamins are raw fruits, raw vegetables, grains, meats, and dairy products.

MINERALS

Some minerals such as Iron, selenium, and sodium are found in the earth. Minerals are called inorganic substance, which the exception of water. Most minerals are essential nutrients, each serving its own purpose. An example would be sodium, which helps to regulate water balance in your body. Minerals are not used as an energy source but help with energy producing- reactions.

All foods contain minerals so if you eat a balanced diet of carbohydrates, fats, and protein, there should be no deficiencies.

UNDERSTANDING THE ENERGY EQUATION

What is energy? Energy is defined as the capacity or power to do work, such as moving an object by the use of force. Understanding the energy equation will help you shed fat and gain muscle faster.

To do physical activity you need energy, which comes from the foods we eat. Throughout this chapter, we will be going through energy balance, how it affects body weight, and energy expenditure.

Energy balance is a state in which energy intake equals the energy burned. An example would be if a person were to eat 2000 calories a day and then burn 2000 calories that same day. Energy imbalances happen when the amount of energy consumed does not equal the amount of energy used.

Energy balance is a state in which energy intake equals the energy burned. An example would be if a person were to eat 2000 calories a day and then burn 2000 calories that same day. Energy imbalances happen when the amount of energy consumed does not equal the amount of energy used.

Energy imbalances result in a positive or negative energy imbalance. Positive energy imbalance is a state where energy intake is greater than the energy expenditure. An example of a positive energy imbalance would be a person eating 3000calories and sitting down all day and watching television burning only 1200calories. Negative energy balance is when energy intake is less that the energy expenditure. An example of negative energy balance is when a person eats 1000 calories and exercises for 3hours and walks around all day burning 1100 calories.

Understanding energy intake and expenditure is one way to keep the body weight stable. When energy intake equals energy expenditure, the body weight becomes stable. In a state of positive energy balance, the body weight increases. When energy intake is in a negative balance, the body weight decreases.

During positive energy balance a person either gains body fat or muscle mass and this depends of what type of activity they are engaging in. Gaining body weight is considered healthy during growth periods during infancy, childhood, and pregnancy.

What is not considered healthy is when a person is in a positive energy balance from being inactive and gains excessive body fat.

Why do people eat food other than for survival and for enjoyment? Hunger and satiety are somewhat complex physiological states that influence the amount of food a person eats. Satiety is a state in which hunger is satisfied and a person feels that they had enough to eat. Hunger is defined as the physiological drive to consume food. Both hunger and satiety are influenced by factors such as gastric (stomach) stretching, circulation nutrient level, and gastrointestinal hormones.

What is a food craving?

A food craving is a very strong desire for a particular food and is different from hunger. Simply put, a food craving is satisfied when the person eats that desired food. Women seem to experience more food cravings then men do. This could be due to the hormonal changes during their menstrual cycles.

During pregnancy, the fluctuations of hormones may cause some women to crave certain foods. Following an over-restrictive diet could also cause food cravings. When I used to diet for bodybuilding competitions, I would restrict sugars, salt, carbs, and certain kinds of fats for 10 weeks. After 2-3 weeks of eating a restrictive diet I would crave certain foods like burgers and chocolate bars. To keep on track and to defeat these food cravings I would allow myself a cheat meal once a week. This would allow me to look forward to that certain day where I would be able to eat whatever I was craving. This is an effective way to stay on track with your eating guidelines if your goal is to lose body fat. Getting enough sleep, exercising regularly, eating a wide variety of healthy foods are other factors to help these food cravings.

We have gone over energy in and energy out, however energy intake is only half of the energy balance equation.

The other half is called energy expenditure. The components that make up energy expenditure are basal metabolism, physical activity, and the thermic effect of food. The thermic effect of food is the energy required to process food and is roughly 10% of total energy expenditure (TEE). Physical energy is the energy required for body movement and is about 15% to 30% of TEE. Basal metabolism is the energy required for basic life function and is roughly 50% to 70% of TEE.

The basal metabolism is the biggest factor of all 3, so the best way to increase your metabolism is building your muscle mass through resistance training.

Muscle mass burns more calories at rest than fat mass.

Most health practitioners know what BMR is and use it to assess people. Basal metabolic rate is the energy used for basal metabolism, which is expressed as kcal per hour. In simple terms, BMR is the amount of calories a person burns at rest.

BMR accounts for 50-70% of TEE and is measured in the morning, during a fasted state, after 8 hours of sleep, and in a temperature controlled room.

Trying to figure out a person's BMR can be a challenge since it requires so many conditions to gather an accurate reading, clinicians often measure resting metabolic rate instead (RMR). RMR is around 10% higher than BMR. When resting metabolism is used over a 24-hour period, it is called resting energy expenditure (REE).

To figure out a person's REE, clinicians use a formula called the Harris Benedict equation, as shown below. If you don't want to calculate it manually, you can always Google the Harris Benedict equation and punch in the numbers.

Males: REE = 66.5 + [13.8 x weight (kg)] + [5 x height (cm)] - [6.8 x age (y)]

Females: REE = 655.1 + [9.6 x weight (kg)] + [1.8 x height (cm)] - [4.7 x age (y)]

As we age, our ability to burn the same amount of calories at rest declines about 2- 5% every 10 years. Add menopause for females, and male pattern baldness to the mix and it doesn't sound like too much fun at all. People with more muscle mass usually have a higher BMR than people with more fat mass. This is because muscle has greater metabolic activity than fat tissue.

As we age, our muscle mass also decreases. These reasons and more are why a person should always include resistance training in their training program.

One of the most interesting factors that can affect a person's BMR is food restriction or extreme dieting. When a person restricts calories over a period of time, they will lose both body fat and muscle.

Another thing that can happen is your BMR slowing down in response to a negative energy balance. This is why some people hit a plateau when dieting over a long period of time.

Physical activity is the second largest part of the total energy expenditure equation and makes up 15-30% of the total equation.

Activities like resistance training, biking, swimming, and walking burn more calories than walking.

Body mass and size also influence energy expended during physical activities. Smaller people have less body mass than a larger person so they would naturally burn fewer calories when doing the same exercise such as running.

Lastly, is the thermic effect of food (TEF). TEF is defined as energy expended for the digestion and absorption of nutrients. Some foods like steak require more energy to break down than others.

High fat foods have the lowest TEF while protein has highest TEF. This does not mean to cut out all high fat food and eat all protein and expect to burn more calories.

Thermic effect of food is only 5 to 10% of the total energy equation. All 3 play an important role together in the quest to burn body fat or build muscle.

EATING FOR MUSCULAR GAINS

Most superheroes are known for their super powers and bulging muscles, such as Superman when he picks up a truck. His muscles ripple as he exerts force.

Muscle translates to physical power and strength. People work out to feel healthier, stronger, and to live a longer life. As we have learned before, our muscle mass declines as we age. A person who carries more muscle mass will burn more calories at rest verses a person with average muscle mass. Most men and even some women who weight train want to look physically powerful.

Did you know around 3500 calories equals to one pound of body weight? Going back to the male who is 35 and has a BMR of 1706 kcal per day. The BMR can be used as a base for muscle gain and fat loss. Once a person has established their BMR, it is crucial they stay in the positive energy balance to gain weight.

The next step is to look at your caloric intake. Once you have figured out your caloric intake, it must be greater than your BMR. Weight training sessions can burn up 200-300 calories per session depending on the intensity level. So 2-3 weight training sessions a week would be an extra 600-900 extra calories on top of the 1706. That would bring the caloric intake up between 2306 and 2606 calories. I would then add an extra 400 calories to be in the positive energy balance making total caloric intake between 2706 and 3006. An easier way to do this is to google TDEE calculator. If we were to use the same person who has the BMR of 1706, his TDEE would be 2906 calories. In order to gain muscle naturally a person must gain some body fat also.

Some experts say 1 pound of muscle for every 2-3 lbs of fat but everyone is different so there is no exact number. It is impossible to gain pure muscle mass unless the person is chemically enhanced. Chemically enhanced means the use steroids, growth hormone, clenburatol, and a list of other various drugs.

In order to lose body fat a person must follow a diet of clean eating and caloric reduction. One example of clean protein source would be a grilled chicken breast with lemon, salt, and garlic. A bad choice would be deep-fried chicken or deep-fried, battered fish. In order to gain muscle a person must follow a higher caloric diet, so eating a cheat meal more frequently is not a bad idea. When losing body fat, it is crucial to eat clean 80-90 percent of the time but when gaining muscle a person can cheat more frequently since their calories are not as restrictive.

One of the most talked about issues when trying to add muscle mass is the protein intake and what is the proper amount. As I said before someone who is active should consume between 1.6 to 2.2 grams per kilo/day. So a person who weighs 75 kg would consume between 120-165 grams per day. If a person were to eat 3 small meals and 3 snacks a day, this would work out roughly to 20-27.5 grams of protein per meal. Using these numbers as a guide, I would round it up to 30 grams per meal.

When building muscle, it is important to also eat enough carbohydrates and fats. If a good ratio to follow is 30% protein, 50% carbohydrates, and 20% fat. If you find you're gaining too much fat, you can cut back on the carbs by 10% and increase the ratio of protein by 10%. A person eating 3000 calories a day at 30/50/20 would have the following ratio breakdowns. Protein breakdown would be 900 (3000x.30) calories and would be 225 (900/4) grams per day. The person would consume 37.5 grams per meal if they were to eat 6 times in a day. Carbohydrates would be 1500 (3000x.5) calories and would be 375 (1500/4) grams per day. The person would eat 62.5 (375/4) grams per meal if they were to eat 6 times in a day. Fats would be 600 (3000x.2) calories and would be 67 (600/9) grams per day. The person would consume 11 (67/9) grams per meal if they were to eat 6 times in a day.

After a person weight trains, it is best they consume some post-workout food or a post-workout shake. I always have a protein and carbohydrate shake after I weight train. The shake consists of 60-80 grams of carbohydrates and 40-50 grams of protein.

When a person weight trains they rip the muscle and use up their stored glycogen inside of the muscle. So the carbohydrates are used to replenish the lost glycogen and the protein is used to repair the muscle. It is best to have a shake or meal within 30-40 minutes after training.

The last thing a person wants is to let the body starve and turn on itself for the missing nutrients. A post-workout shake for males should consist of 50-60 grams of carbs after and 40-50 grams of protein after.

A post-workout shake for females should consist of 20-30 grams of carbs and 20-30 grams of protein after. To keep things simple, any protein powder works and any fast-acting carbohydrates that is high on the GI charts.

Carbohydrates like white rice, instant oatmeal, cornflakes, and sugars. If a person where to choose a protein food source, they should stick to faster digesting proteins like chicken, turkey, and fish.

These are just guidelines to follow but the main point to is keep a positive energy intake when trying to build muscle mass. If you are unsure of what to eat go back and read the protein, fat, and carbohydrate chapters over again.

If you are starting to look like a good year blimp from all the extra calories add some cardiovascular workouts to your schedule or change the protein and carbohydrate ratio. There is no real secret to gaining muscle but being consistent with your eating, sleeping, and training.

TOP 5 RULES FOR GAINING MUSCLE

Here are the top rules for gaining size. I wish I had this knowledge when I started training at 18. I would have been able to add more quality size faster.

1. Never let yourself get hungry. You need a consistent flow of nutrients to your muscles all the time when building bulk. Have snacks around you all the time. Snacks like protein bars, nuts, and cheese. Stuff your face like a chipmunk.

2. Train heavy or increase the volume of force on your muscles. Your muscles grow from extra stress that comes from heavier weight or increased volume.

3. Get adequate rest in between your workouts and at night. Your muscles grow when you rest. Do not over train as this is counterproductive to growth. If you have not fully recovered from your previous workout, take another day off. More is not always better.

4. Do not stop cardiovascular workouts completely. When people bulk up, they often neglect cardio. Just cut down on the volume and intensity of those types of workouts. Just do light walking instead of running. Doing light cardio will help with keeping your BMR up which will help burn more calories efficiently.

5. The top 5 supplements to use when bulking are creatine hydrochloride (HCL), weight gainers, glutamine, vitamins (if needed), and whey or isolate protein powder.

TWO DIET EXAMPLES OF EATING PLANS FOR GAINING MUSCLE

EATING PLAN 1

This is an example of a diet for a male who does not have as much time to eat, slower metabolism, but still wants to gain muscle mass.

He would eat 3 meals and 2 snacks. Please see next page.

Meal 1 8:00am	2 slices whole grain toast with 2 tsp. natural peanut butter 2 whole eggs with ketchup and cheese 1 cup of carrots 1 medium pear
Meal 2 12:00pm	7-8oz salmon with lemon, garlic, brown sugar 2 cups of Caesar salad 1 large potato with cheese and butter
Snack 1 3:00pm	2 promax or quest protein bars
Meal 3 6:00pm	7-8oz steak with steak sauce 2 cups pasta with spaghetti sauce 2 cups kale and lettuce with Italian salad dressing
Snack 2 8:30pm	5-6 oz protein source 1 cup of fruit yogurt or 2 cups of cottage cheese

EATING PLAN 2

This is a variation for a female who would want to gain some muscle or who has a fast metabolism and needs to put on some body weight.

Most females want to lose weight but there are some who have an extremely fast metabolism and gaining muscle is quite a challenge.

I have trained over a few hundred females so I have come across every type of body and metabolism type. Please see next page.

Meal 1 8:00am	whole egg with 1 egg white and cheese 1 slice of whole grain toast tsp. natural peanut butter or jam 1/2 cup of grapes
Meal 2 12:00pm	3-4oz chicken with barbecue sauce 1 cup steamed broccoli 1 cup brown rice with soya sauce
Snack 1 3:00pm	1 scoop whey isolate 1 cup fruit yogurt
Meal 3 6:00pm	3-4oz lean ground turkey with curry sauce 1.5 cup of mixed salad with Greek dressing 1/2 yam or small baked potato with cheese and butter
Snack 2 8:30pm	1/2 avocado 2-3oz fish or 1/2 cup unsalted nuts 1 cup fruit yogurt

5 HIGH CALORIE PROTEIN SHAKES

In the quest to build muscle mass taking in those extra calories is important for recovery and growth.

When you are eating over 4000 calories, high calorie protein shakes are a good option.

Here are 5 high calorie protein shakes to incorporate into your bulking diet.

1. High Protein Milkshake

1 cup whole milk
1 scoop whey protein powder
1/4 cup dry milk powder
3/4 cup ice cream

Add ice cream, protein powder, and milk powder to milk and beat well.

Calories = 533

Protein= 36

2. Strawberry Yogurt Frost

1 envelope strawberry instant breakfast
1 scoop whey protein powder
1 cup whole milk
1/4 cup dry milk powder
1/3 cup strawberry yogurt
6 ice cubes

Combine all ingredients in a blender. Blend until smooth.

Calories = 524

Protein = 41

3. OJ and Cinnamon Smoothie

1 envelope vanilla instant breakfast
1 scoop whey protein powder
1 cup whole milk
1/4 cup dry milk powder
3 Tbs thawed orange juice concentrate
1/8 tsp ground cinnamon

6 ice cubes

Combine all ingredients in a blender. Blend until smooth.

Calories = 537

Protein = 38

4. Mocha-Banana Shake

1 envelope chocolate instant breakfast
1 scoop whey protein powder
1 cup whole milk
1/4 cup dry milk powder
1 medium ripe banana
1/2 tsp instant coffee crystals

Combine all ingredients in a blender. Blend until smooth.

Calories = 542

Protein = 39

5. Hawaiian Slush

6 oz. Hawaiian Punch
1 scoop whey protein powder
1/3 cup dry milk powder
1/2 cup lemon sherbet
1 Tbs sugar
3 ice cubes

Combine all ingredients in a blender and blend for about 10 seconds. Fruit juice can be used in place of the Hawaiian Punch.

Calories = 415

Protein = 28

WHAT ARE YOUR GOALS

What are your goals?

Do you want to gain 5 lbs, 10lbs, or bench press your body weight?

Write down some of your goals below.

Remember to be realistic as building muscle takes time. If you set 3 small goals to gain 5 lbs, that equates to an overall gain of 15lbs.

1.

2.

3.

4.

5.

TRAINING GUIDELINES

Read and memorize this before you start your training program.

1. Always practice good form. A good controlled set will recruit more muscle fibers verses throwing the weights around.

2. Do one warm up set with a lighter weight. This will allow you to practice the exercise and execute good form for the next sets.

3. Lower the weight in a controlled manner. The lowering part of the rep is called the negative (eccentric) portion. More control in the lowering portion will recruit more muscle fibers.

4. Breathe out with force. Never hold your breath during a set. Your muscles need oxygen to keep working and to expel carbon dioxide. A red face does not look attractive.

5. Know when to stop. Sometimes it is not good to push beyond failure. Pushing yourself to hard all the time can lead to injuries.

6. Record your weights in a book to track your progress. This is how to track your progress. In the paperback edition, you will be able to write the weight right beside the exercise.

7. Do large muscle groups before smaller muscle groups as they require the most energy. Doing biceps before training your back is detrimental to your back workout as your arms will fatigue first.

8. Always set goals before you start any training program. This will give you more purpose and will help you reach your goal.

9. Try not to grunt or scream when you do your set or reps. Save your energy for the next set. You are not impressing anyone.

10. If you are unsure of any exercises just look them up in the internet. Study the form of every exercise.

11. Weigh yourself once a week at the same time and day. Preferably in the morning before you eat breakfast.

TWO WEEK BEGINNER TRAINING PROGRAM

Are you a beginner and have no training experience?

If you answered yes, just follow this two week program as a warm up. Learn all the exercises and then proceed to the eight week training program after.

Week 1

Sunday: Rest

Monday: Workout 1 (full body workout)

Tuesday: Rest

Wednesday: Cardio + core (abs)

Thursday: Workout 2 (full body workout)

Friday: Rest

Saturday: Light cardio

Monday

Workout 1

1. Warm up for 5-6 minutes on a cardio machine

2. Lat pull down to front – 1x12, 1x10, 1x8 reps

3. Machine leg press – 1x12, 1x10, 1x8 reps

4. Machine back row – 1x12, 1x10, 1x8 reps

5. Machine bench press – 1x12, 1x10, 1x8 reps

6. Lying prone machine hamstring curls – 1x12, 1x10, 1x8 reps

7. Machine shoulder press – 1x12, 1x10, 1x8 reps

8. Seated adductor machine – 1x15, 1x12, 1x10 reps

9. Cool down for 5-6 minutes on a cardio machine

10. Static stretching or use my stretching app

Wednesday

Cardio – 20 minutes

1. Bike – 10 minutes

2. Treadmill – 10 minutes

Core

1. Bird dogs - 1 x12, 1x12 reps

2. Seated leg lifts – 1x15, 1x15 for each side

3. Cable crunches - 1x15, 1x15 reps

4. Standing medicine ball twists – 1 minute

Thursday

Workout 2

1. Warm up for 5-6 minutes on a cardio machine

2. Reverse grip bar pull downs – 1x15, 1x12, 1x10 reps

3. Seated machine leg extensions – 1x15, 1x12, 1x10 reps

4. Pulley low grip back rows – 1x15, 1x12, 1x10 reps

5. Flat dumbbell chest fly – 1x15, 1x12, 1x10 reps

6. Seated upright hamstring curls – 1x15, 1x12, 1x10 reps

7. Dumbbell side laterals – 1x15, 1x12, 1x10 reps

8. Seal jacks – 1x15, 1x15 reps

9. Machine triceps extension – 1x15, 1x12, 1x10 reps

10. Machine biceps curls – 1x15, 1x10 reps

11. Cool down for 5-6 minutes on a cardio machine

12. Static stretching or use my stretching app

https://goo.gl/RLSCHo

Saturday

Cardio – 20 minutes

1. Elliptical – 10 minutes

2. Rowing – 10 minutes

Core

1. Hold superman – 1x15, 1x15 seconds

2. Standing bicycle crunches – 1x15, 1x15 reps

3. Oblique cable twists – 1x15, 1x15 each side

EIGHT WEEK STRENGTH TRAINING PROGRAM FOR MEN

If you have completed the two week beginner program, you are now ready for the eight week training program.

If you are not a beginner, just jump into this training program.

Get ready to grow and train!

8 Week Strength & Mass Building Program For Men – Level 1

Week 1: Heavy week

1. Figure out your 1RM (rep max) and then go up to 90% of your 1RM on your last set.

- a 200 lb bench press would be 180 for the last set of 4 reps

2. Figure out your BMR (basal metabolic rate) and then add 500-600 calories extra per day.

- total caloric intake for the week 500 x 7 = 3500 extra calories

- another easier method is to use TDEE which was explained earlier

3. Always do a 5-8 minute warm-up and 5-8 minute cool down before and after every training session.

This should include static stretching after each exercise session.

4. Use ascending pyramiding for all set and exercises throughout this program.

5. If you are unsure of any exercise just look it up on the internet.

6. Rest 30-60 seconds in between all sets and reps.

7. Go to failure on the last set and record all your weights.

Sunday: Cardio 20-25 minutes + core

Monday: Back + hamstrings

Tuesday: Chest + triceps

Wednesday: Rest day

Thursday: Shoulders + biceps + forearms + core

Friday: Quadriceps + calves + traps

Saturday: Rest day

Sunday

Cardio

1. Bike or tread mile - 20-25 minutes

Core

1. Hold Superman - 1 x 15, 1x15 seconds

2. Scissor kicks – 1x15, 1x15, 1x15 reps

3. Dumbbell crunches – 1x15, 1x15, 1x15 reps

4. Side planks - 1 x 15 seconds each side

Monday

Back

1. Deadlifts - 1x10, 1x8, 1x6 reps

2. Reverse grip pull downs - 1x10, 1x8, 1x6 reps

3. Barbell back rows - 1x10, 1x8, 1x6 reps

4. Pulley seated back rows - 1x10, 1x8, 1x6 reps

Hamstrings

1. Lying leg curls - 1x10, 1x8, 1x6 reps

2. Stiff legged dead lifts - 1x10, 1x8, 1x6 reps

Tuesday

Chest

1. Incline bench press - 1x10, 1x8, 1x6 reps

2. Flat bench press - 1x10, 1x8, 1x6 reps

3. Dumbbell pullovers - 1x10, 1x8, 1x6 reps

Triceps

1. Bar pulley push downs - 1x10, 1x8, 1x6 reps

2. Pulley rope overhead extensions - 1x10, 1x8 reps

3. W-bar skull crushers - 1x10, 1x8 reps

Thursday

Shoulders

1. Seated barbell front press - 1x10, 1x8, 1x6 reps

2. Dumbbell side laterals - 1x10, 1x8, 1x6 reps

3. Bent over dumbbell rear laterals - 1x10, 1x8, 1x6 reps

Biceps

1. Barbell biceps curls - 1x10, 1x8, 1x6 reps

2. Seated machine biceps curls - 1x10, 1x8, 1x6 reps

Forearms

1. Behind the body bar curls - 1x10, 1x8 reps

2. Standing reverse bar curls - 1x10, 1x8 reps

Core

1. Same core as Sunday workout

Friday

Quadriceps

1. Plate loader leg press - 1x10, 1x8, 1x6, 1x4 reps

2. Back squats - 1x10, 1x8, 1x6, 1x4 reps

3. Leg extensions - 1x10, 1x8, 1x6, 1x4 reps

Calves

1. Seated calf raises - 1x12, 1x10, 1x8 reps

2. Standing calf raises - 1x12, 1x10, 1x8 reps

Traps

Dumbbell shrugs - 1x10, 1x8, 1x6 reps

Week 2: Medium Light Week

1. Go up to 70% 1RM

- a 200 lb bench press would be 140 for 8 reps on the last set

2. Do not go to failure on any set

Sunday: Cardio 20-25 minutes + core

Monday: Chest + back

Tuesday: Shoulders + hamstrings

Wednesday: Rest

Thursday: Quadriceps + adductors + abductors + calves + traps

Friday: Triceps + biceps + forearms + core

Sat: Rest

Sunday

Cardio

1. Tread mile or elliptical - 20-25 minutes

Core

1. Back extensions on the mat – 1x15, 1x15 reps

2. Reverse crunches – 1x12, 1x12, 1x12 reps

3. Cable crunches – 1x12, 1x12, 1x12 reps

4. Dumbbell side tilts - 1x15 each side

Monday

Chest

1. Regular pushups - 1x15, 1x15, 1x15 reps

2. Incline dumbbell chest press - 1x15, 1x12, 1x10 reps

3. Cable crossovers - 1x15, 1x12, 1x10 reps

Back

1. Seated machine back row - 1x15, 1x12, 1x10 reps

2. Close grip pull down - 1x15, 1x12, 1x10 reps

3. One arm dumbbell back rows - 1x15, 1x12, 1x10 reps

4. High pulley pullovers - 1x15, 1x12, 1x10 reps

Tuesday

Shoulders

1. Machine shoulder press - 1x15, 1x12, 1x10 reps

2. Barbell upright rows - 1x15, 1x12, 1x10 reps

3. Pulley face pulls - 1x15, 1x12, 1x10 reps

Hamstrings

1. Seated hamstring curls - 1x15, 1x12, 1x10 reps

2. Dumbbell dead lifts - 1x15, 1x12, 1x10 reps

Thursday

Quadriceps/abductors/adductors

1. Leg extensions - 1x15, 1x12, 1x10 reps

2. Plie dumbbell squats - 1x15, 1x12, 1x10 reps

3. Seated adductor machine - 1x15, 1x12 reps

4. Seated abductor machine - 1x15, 1x12 reps

5. Bulgarian split squats - 1x15, 1x12, 1x10 for each leg

Calves

1. One legged standing dumbbell calf raises - 1x15, 1x12, 1x10 for each side

2. Seated calf raises - 1x15, 1x12, 1x10 reps

Traps

1. Barbell shrugs - 1x15, 1x12, 1x10 reps

Friday

Triceps

1. Close grip bench presses - 1x15, 1x12, 1x10 reps

2. One arm overhead dumbbell triceps extension - 1x15, 1x12 each side

3. One arm dumbbell triceps kickbacks - 1x15, 1x12 each side

Biceps

1. Alternate dumbbell bicep curls - 1x15, 1x12, 1x10 reps

2. Preacher curls - 1x15, 1x12, 1x10 reps

Forearms

1. Reverse preacher curls - 1x15, 1x12 reps

2. Seated dumbbell palms up wrist curls - 1x15, 1x12 reps

Core

1. Same core as Sunday

Week 3: Heavy Week

1. Go up 5-10 lbs from week 1 on all exercises

2. A 5 lb increase on smaller muscle groups and a 10 lb increase on larger muscle groups

3. Go to failure on the last set

Sunday: Cardio 20-25 minutes + core

Monday: Back + hamstrings

Tuesday: Chest + triceps

Wed: Rest

Thursday: Shoulders + biceps + forearms + core

Friday: Quadriceps + calves + traps

Saturday: Rest

Sunday

Cardio

1. Tread mile or rowing machine - 20-25 minutes

Core

1. Single prone leg lifts - 1x12, 1x12 each leg

2. Bicycles - 1x15, 1x15, 1x15 reps

3. Side plank reaches - 1x10 each side

Monday

Back

1. Barbell back rows - 1x12, 1x10, 1x8 reps

2. Reverse grip pull downs - 1x12, 1x10, 1x8 reps

3. Bar deadlifts - 1x12, 1x10, 1x8 reps

4. Chin ups - 1x12, 1x10, 1x8 reps (use chin up assisted machine)

Hamstrings

1. Lying leg curls - 1x12, 1x10, 1x8 reps

2. Seated leg curls - 1x12, 1x10, 1x8 reps

Tuesday

Chest

1. Flat bench press - 1x12, 1x10, 1x8 reps

2. Incline bench press - 1x12, 1x10, 1x8 reps

3. Incline dumbbell fly - 1x12, 1x10, 1x8 reps

Triceps

1. Bar skull crushers - 1x12, 1x10, 1x8 reps

2. Pulley push downs - 1x12, 1x10 reps

3. Pulley rope triceps overhead extensions - 1x12, 1x10 reps

Thursday

Shoulders

1. Dumbbell side laterals - 1x12, 1x10, 1x8 reps

2. Seated barbell front shoulder press - 1x12, 1x10, 1x8 reps

3. Bent over dumbbell rear laterals raises- 1x12, 1x10, 1x8 reps

Biceps

1. Seated machine biceps curls - 1x12, 1x10, 1x8 reps

2. Barbell biceps curls - 1x12, 1x10, 1x8 reps

Forearms

1. Standing reverse curls - 1x12, 1x10 reps

2. Behind the body curls - 1x12, 1x10 reps

Core

1. Same workout as Sunday

Friday

Quadriceps

1. Back squats - 1x12, 1x10, 1x8 reps

2. Leg press - 1x12, 1x10, 1x8 reps

3. Leg extensions - 1x12, 1x10, 1x8 reps

4. Hack squats - 1x12, 1x10, 1x8 reps

Calves

1. Standing calf raises - 1x12, 1x10, 1x8 reps

2. Seated calf raises - 1x12, 1x10, 1x8 reps

Traps

Dumbbell shrugs - 1x12, 1x10, 1x8 reps

Week 4: Medium - Light week

1. Keep the same weights as week 2

2. We are increasing the resistance by increasing the reps

3. Do not go to failure for any sets

Sunday: Cardio 20-25 minutes + core

Monday: Chest + back

Tuesday: Shoulders + hamstrings

Wednesday: Rest

Thursday: Quadriceps + adductors + abductors + traps + calves

Friday: Triceps + biceps + forearms + core

Saturday: Rest

Sunday

Cardio

1. Treadmill or elliptical - 20-25 minutes

Core

1. Bird dogs - 1x15, 1x15 reps

2. Dumbbell side tilts - 1x15 each side

3. Stability ball passes - 1x10, 1x10, 1x10 reps

Monday

Back

1. Close grip V-bar pull down - 1x20, 1x15, 1x12 reps

2. Machine back row - 1x20, 1x15, 1x12 reps

3. High pulley pullovers - 1x20, 1x15, 1x12 reps

4. One arm dumbbell rows - 1x20, 1x15, 1x12 reps

Chest

1. Incline dumbbell chest press - 1x20, 1x15, 1x12 reps

2. Regular pushups - 1x15, 1x15, 1x15 reps

3. Cable crossovers - 1x20, 1x15, 1x12 reps

Tuesday

Shoulders

1. Machine shoulder press - 1x20, 1x15, 1x12 reps

2. Pulley face pulls - 1x20, 1x15, 1x12 reps

3. Barbell upright rows - 1x20, 1x15, 1x12 reps

Hamstrings

1. Dumbbell stiff legged dead lifts - 1x20, 1x15, 1x12 reps

2. Seated hamstring curls - 1x20, 1x15, 1x12 reps

Thursday

Quadriceps/adductors/abductors

1. Leg extensions - 1x20, 1x15, 1x12 reps

2. Bulgarian split squats - 1x20, 1x15, 1x12 for each leg

3. Seated adductor machine - 1x20, 1x15 reps

4. Seated abductor machine - 1x20, 1x15 reps

5. Plie dumbbell squats - 1x20, 1x15, 1x12 reps

Calves

1. Seated calf raises - 1x20, 1x15, 1x12 reps

2. One legged standing dumbbell calf raises - 1x20, 1x15, 1x12 for each side

Traps

1. Barbell shrugs - 1x20, 1x15, 1x12 reps

Friday

Triceps

1. Seated overhead dumbbell triceps extensions - 1x20, 1x15, 1x12 reps

2. Close grip bench presses - 1x20, 1x15 reps

3. One arm dumbbell kickbacks - 1x20, 1x15 reps

Biceps

1. Preacher bar bicep curls - 1x20, 1x15, 1x10 reps

2. Alternate dumbbell biceps curls - 1x20, 1x15, 1x10 reps

Forearms

1. Seated palms up wrist curls - 1x20, 1x15 reps

2. Reverse preacher curls - 1x20, 1x15 reps

Core

1. Same workout as Sunday

Week 5: Heavy Week

1. Figure out your 1RM

2. Go to up to 90% of your 1RM for all exercises.

3. Go to failure for the last set.

Sunday: Cardio 20-25 minutes + core

Monday: Chest + triceps

Tuesday: Back + biceps

Wednesday: Rest

Thursday: Shoulders + traps + forearms + core

Friday: Quadriceps +hamstrings+ calves

Saturday: Rest

Sunday

Cardio

1. Elliptical or Rower - 20-25 minutes

Core

1. Hold superman – 1x15, 1x15 seconds

2. Dumbbell crunches – 1x15, 1x15, 1x15 reps

3. Scissor kicks – 1x15, 1x15, 1x15 reps

4. Side planks – 1x15 seconds each side

Monday

Chest

1. Flat dumbbell bench press - 1x10, 1x8, 1x6 reps

2. Machine chest fly - 1x10, 1x8, 1x6 reps

3. Incline dumbbell bench press - 1x10, 1x8, 1x6 reps

Triceps

1. Rope triceps push downs - 1x10, 1x8, 1x6 reps

2. Decline dumbbell triceps extensions - 1x10, 1x8 reps

3. Mini-dips - 1x10, 1x8 reps

Tuesday

Back

1. Close grip v-bar pull downs - 1x10, 1x8, 1x6 reps

2. Seated v-bar back pulley rows - 1x10, 1x8, 1x6 reps

3. Under grip chin ups - 1x10, 1x8, 1x6 reps

4. One arm dumbbell back rows - 1x10, 1x8, 1x6 reps

Biceps

1. Machine biceps curls - 1x10, 1x8, 1x6 reps

2. Incline dumbbell biceps curls - 1x10, 1x8, 1x6 reps

Thursday

Shoulders

1. Seated dumbbell shoulder presses - 1x10, 1x8, 1x6 reps

2. Cable side laterals - 1x10, 1x8, 1x6 reps

3. Machine rear delt fly - 1x10, 1x8, 1x6 reps

Traps

1. Barbell shrugs - 1x10, 1x8, 1x6 reps

Forearms

1. Dumbbell hammer curls - 1x10, 1x8, 1x6 reps

2. Behind the body curls - 1x10, 1x8, 1x6 reps

Core

1. Same as Sunday

Friday

Quadriceps

1. Back squats - 1x10, 1x8, 1x6 reps

2. Leg extensions - 1x10, 1x8, 1x6 reps

3. Machine leg press - 1x10, 1x8, 1x6 reps

4. Single leg extensions - 1x10, 1x8, 1x6 reps

Hamstrings

1. Standing leg curls - 1x10, 1x8 1x6 reps

2. Lying leg curls - 1x10, 1x8, 1x6 reps

Calves

1. Leg press machine calf pushes - 1x12, 1x10, 1x8 reps

2. Seated calf raises - 1x12, 1x10, 1x8 reps

Week 6: Medium Light Week

1. Go up 5 lbs for small muscle groups from week 4

2. Go up 10 lbs for larger muscle groups from week 4

3. Do not go to failure on any set

Sunday: Cardio 20-25 minutes + core

Monday: Chest + quadriceps

Tuesday: Shoulders + triceps

Wednesday: Rest

Thursday: Back + hamstrings

Friday: Traps + biceps + forearms + core

Saturday: Rest

Sunday

Cardio

1. Tread mile or bike - 20-25 minutes

Core

1. On stomach back extensions - 1x15, 1x15 reps

2. Cable crunches - 1x15, 1x15, 1x15 reps

3. Reverse crunches - 1x15, 1x15, 1x15 reps

4. Dumbbell side tilts - 1x15, 1x15 each side

Monday

Chest

1. Incline dumbbell flye - 1x15, 1x12, 1x10 reps

2. Flat machine bench press - 1x15, 1x12, 1x10 reps

3. Machine chest fly - 1x15, 1x12, 1x10 reps

Quadriceps

1. Holding dumbbell squats - 1x15, 1x12, 1x10 reps

2. Leg extensions - 1x15, 1x12, 1x10 reps

3. Side lunges on bosu - 1x15, 1x15, 1x15 for each side

4. Hack squats - 1x15, 1x12, 1x10 reps

Tuesday

Shoulders

1. Dumbbell front laterals - 1x15, 1x12, 1x10 reps

2. Dumbbell side laterals - 1x15, 1x12, 1x10 reps

3. Dumbbell rear laterals - 1x15, 1x12, 1x10 reps

Triceps

1. W-bar skull crushers - 1x15, 1x12, 1x10 reps

2. Rope pulley overhead triceps extensions - 1x15, 1x12 reps

3. Triceps dip machine - 1x15, 1x12 reps

Thursday

Back

1. T-bar rows - 1x15, 1x12, 1x10 reps

2. Seated back pulley rows - 1x15, 1x12, 1x10 reps

3. Pull down to front - 1x15, 1x12, 1x10 reps

4. Under grip pull downs - 1x15, 1x12, 1x10 reps

Hamstrings

1. Supine one legged ball curls - 1x10, 1x10, 1x10 for each leg

2. Dumbbell stiff legged dead lifts - 1x15, 1x12, 1x10 reps

Calves

1. Seated calf raises - 1x15, 1x12, 1x10 reps

2. Plate loader leg press calf pushes - 1x15, 1x12, 1x10 reps

Friday

Traps

1. Dumbbell shrugs - 1x15, 1x12, 1x10, 1x8 reps

Biceps

1. Bar pulley biceps curls - 1x15, 1x12, 1x10 reps

2. Pulley overhead cable curls - 1x15, 1x12, 1x10 reps

Forearms

1. Reverse barbell curls - 1x15, 1x12 reps

2. Cross the bench bar flexor curls - 1x15, 1x12 reps

Core

1. Same as Sunday workout

Week 7: Heavy Week

1. Go up 5lbs for smaller muscle groups from week 5

2. Go up 10 lbs for larger muscle groups from week 5

3. Go to failure for the last set

Sunday: Cardio + core

Monday: Chest + triceps

Tuesday: Back + biceps

Wednesday: Rest

Thursday: Shoulders + traps + forearms + core

Friday: Quadriceps + hamstrings + calves

Saturday: Rest

Sunday

Cardio

1. Rower or Tread mile - 20-25 minutes

Core

1. Single prone leg lifts - 1x15, 1x15 each leg

2. Elbow plank - 30 seconds x2

3. V-sit holds – 30 seconds x2

4. Standing medicine ball twists - 1 minute

Monday

Chest

1. Incline dumbbell chest press - 1x12, 1x10, 1x8 reps

2. Machine chest fly - 1x12, 1x10, 1x8 reps

3. Flat dumbbell bench press - 1x12, 1x10, 1x8 reps

Triceps

1. Rope triceps push downs - 1x12, 1x10, 1x8 reps

2. Partial mini- dips - 1x12, 1x10 reps

3. Decline dumbbell triceps extensions - 1x12, 1x10 reps

Tuesday

Back

1. Close grip V-bar pull down - 1x12, 1x10, 1x8 reps

2. One arm back dumbbell rows - 1x12, 1x10, 1x8 reps

3. Under grip chin ups - 1x12, 1x10, 1x8 reps

4. Seated V-bar back pulley rows - 1x12, 1x10, 1x8 reps

Biceps

1. Incline dumbbell curls - 1x12, 1x10, 1x8 reps

2. Machine biceps curls - 1x12, 1x10, 1x8 reps

Thursday

Shoulders

1. Cable side laterals - 1x12, 1x10, 1x8 reps

2. Dumbbell shoulder presses - 1x12, 1x10, 1x8 reps

3. Machine rear delt fly - 1x12, 1x10, 1x8 reps

Traps

1. Barbell shrugs - 1x12, 1x10, 1x8 reps

Forearms

1. Behind the body bar curls - 1x12, 1x10 reps

2. Dumbbell hammer curls - 1x12, 1x10 reps

Core

1. Same workout as Sunday

Friday

Quadriceps

1. Machine leg press - 1x12, 1x10, 1x8 reps

2. Leg extensions - 1x12, 1x10, 1x8 reps

3. Back squats - 1x12, 1x10, 1x8 reps

4. Single leg extensions - 1x12, 1x10 reps

Hamstrings

1. Lying leg curls - 1x12, 1x10, 1x8 reps

2. Standing leg curls, 1x12, 1x10, 1x18 reps

Calves

1. Seated calf raises - 1x12, 1x10, 1x8 reps

2. Leg press calf pushes - 1x12, 1x10, 1x8 reps

Week 8: Light Medium Week

1. Use same weights as week 6 and we will increase resistance by reps

2. Do not go to failure any set

Sunday: Cardio + core

Monday: Chest + quadriceps

Tuesday: Shoulders + triceps

Wednesday: Rest

Thursday: Back + hamstrings + calves

Friday: Traps + biceps + forearms + core

Saturday: Rest

Sunday

Cardio

1. Bike or tread mile - 20-25 minutes

Core

1. Land swimming – 1x15, 1x15 seconds

2. Stability ball pikes – 1x15, 1x15, 1x15 reps

3. Standing oblique bar twists - 1x1 minute

Monday

1. Flat machine bench press - 1x20, 1x15, 1x12 reps

2. Incline dumbbell fly - 1x20, 1x15, 1x12 reps

3. Machine chest fly - 1x20, 1x15, 1x12 reps

Quadriceps

1. Hack squats - 1x20, 1x15, 1x12 reps

2. Leg extensions - 1x20, 1x15, 1x12 reps

3. Holding dumbbell squats - 1x20, 1x15, 1x12 reps

4. Side lunges on bosu - 1x15, 1x15, 1x15 for each side

Tuesday

Shoulders

1. Side laterals - 1x20, 1x15, 1x12 reps

2. Front laterals - 1x20, 1x15, 1x12 reps

3. Rear laterals - 1x20, 1x15, 1x12 reps

Triceps

1. Triceps dip machine - 1x20, 1x15, 1x12 reps

2. Rope overhead triceps extensions - 1x20, 1x15 reps

3. W-bar skull crushers - 1x20, 1x15 reps

Thursday

Back

1. Under grip pull downs - 1x20, 1x15, 1x12 reps

2. Pull down to front - 1x20, 1x15, 1x12 reps

3. T-bar rows - 1x20, 1x15, 1x12 reps

4. Seated back pulley rows - 1x20, 1x15, 1x12 reps

Hamstrings

1. Dumbbell deadlifts - 1x20, 1x15, 1x12 reps

2. Supine hamstring ball curls - 1x15, 1x15, 1x15 reps

Calves

1. Plate loader calf pushes - 1x20, 1x15, 1x12 reps

2. Seated calf raises - 1x20, 1x15, 1x12 reps

Friday

Traps

1. Dumbbell shrugs - 1x20, 1x15, 1x12 reps

Biceps

1. Overhead cable curls - 1x20, 1x15, 1x10 reps

2. Bar pulley curls - 1x20, 1x15, 1x10 reps

Forearms

1. Cross the bench bar flexor curls - 1x20, 1x15 reps

2. Reverse barbell curls - 1x20, 1x15 reps

Core

1. Same workout as Sunday

EIGHT WEEK STRENGTH TRAINING PROGRAM FOR WOMEN

If you have completed the two week warm up program, you are now ready for the eight week training program.

If you are not a beginner, then jump right into this program.

Remember, if the volume of sets and repetitions are too much, then just reduce the amount to suit your individual needs.

Get ready to train and build some muscle!

8 Week Strength & Mass Building Program For Women – Level 1

Week 1: Heavy week

1. Figure out your 1RM (rep max) and then go up to 90% of your 1RM on your last set.

- a 200 lb bench press would be 180 for the last set of 4 reps

2. Figure out your BMR (basal metabolic rate) and add 200-300 calories extra per day.

- total caloric intake for the week 200 x7 = 1400 extra calories

3. Always do a 5-8 minute warm-up and 5-8 minute cool down before and after every training session.

This should include static stretching after each exercise session.

4. Use ascending pyramiding for all set and exercises throughout this program.

5. If you are unsure of any exercise just look it up on the internet.

6. Go to failure on the last set and record all your weights.

7. Rest 30-40 seconds in between on all sets and reps.

Sunday: Cardio 25-30 minutes + core

Monday: Back + hamstrings

Tuesday: Chest + triceps

Wednesday: Rest day

Thursday: Shoulders + biceps + core

Friday: Quadriceps + calves

Saturday: Rest day or light walking

Sunday

Cardio

1. Bike or tread mile – 25-30 minutes

Core

1. Hold Superman – 1x15, 1x15 seconds

2. Scissor kicks – 1x15, 1x15, 1x15 reps

3. Dumbbell crunches – 1x15, 1x15, 1x15 reps

4. Side planks – 1x15, 1x15 seconds each side

Monday

Back

1. Deadlifts - 1x10, 1x8, 1x6 reps

2. Reverse grip pull downs - 1x10, 1x8 reps

3. Barbell back rows - 1x10, 1x8, 1x6 reps

4. Lat pull down to front - 1x10, 1x8, 1x6 reps

Hamstrings

1. Lying leg curls - 1x10, 1x8, 1x6reps

2. Stiff legged dead lifts - 1x10, 1x8, 1x6 reps

Tuesday

Chest

1. Flat bench press - 1x10, 1x8, 1x6 reps

2. Dumbbell pullovers - 1x10, 1x8, 1x6 reps

3. Incline dumbbell fly - 1x10, 1x8, 1x6 reps

Triceps

1. Bar pulley push downs - 1x10, 1x8, 1x6 reps

2. Pulley rope overhead extensions - 1x10, 1x8reps

3. W-bar skull crushers - 1x10, 1x8 reps

Thursday

Shoulders

1. Seated barbell front press - 1x10, 1x8, 1x6 reps

2. Dumbbell side laterals - 1x10, 1x8, 1x6 reps

3. Bent over dumbbell rear laterals - 1x10, 1x8, 1x6 reps

Biceps

1. Barbell biceps curls - 1x10, 1x8, 1x6 reps

2. Seated machine biceps curls - 1x10, 1x8, 1x6 reps

Core

1. Same core as Sunday workout

Friday

Quadriceps

1. Plate loader leg press - 1x10, 1x8, 1x6, reps

2. Back squats - 1x10, 1x8, 1x6 reps

3. Leg extensions - 1x10, 1x8, 1x6 reps

4. Hack squats - 1x10, 1x8, 1x6 reps

Calves

1. Seated calf raises - 1x12, 1x10, 1x8 reps

2. Standing calf raises - 1x12, 1x10, 1x8 reps

Week 2: Medium- Light Week

1. Go up to 70% 1RM

- a 200 lb bench press would be 140 for 8 reps on the last set

2. Do not go to failure on any set

Sunday: Cardio 25-30 minutes + core

Monday: Chest + back

Tuesday: Shoulders + hamstrings + core

Wednesday: Rest

Thursday: Quadriceps + adductors + abductors + glutes + calves

Friday: Triceps + biceps + cardio

Sat: Rest

Sunday

Cardio

1. Tread mile or elliptical - 20-25 minutes

Core

1. Back extensions on the mat – 1x15, 1x15 reps

2. Reverse crunches – 1x15, 1x15, 1x15 reps

3. Cable crunches – 1x15, 1x15, 1x15 reps

4. Dumbbell side tilts - 1x15 each side

Monday

Chest

1. Regular or knee push ups - 1x15, 1x15, 1x15 reps

2. Incline dumbbell chest press - 1x15, 1x12, 1x10 reps

3. Cable crossovers - 1x15, 1x12, 1x10 reps

Back

1. Seated machine back row - 1x15, 1x12, 1x10 reps

2. Close grip pull down - 1x15, 1x12, 1x10 reps

3. One arm dumbbell back rows - 1x15, 1x12, 1x10 reps

4. High pulley pullovers - 1x15, 1x12, 1x10 reps

Tuesday

Shoulders

1. Machine shoulder press - 1x15, 1x12, 1x10 reps

2. Barbell upright rows - 1x15, 1x12, 1x10, 1x8 reps

3. Pulley face pulls - 1x15, 1x12, 1x10 reps

Hamstrings

1. Seated hamstring curls - 1x15, 1x12, 1x10 reps

2. Dumbbell dead lifts - 1x15, 1x12, 1x10 reps

Thursday

Quadriceps/adductors/abductors

1. Leg extensions - 1x15, 1x12, 1x10, 1x4 reps

2. Plie dumbbell squats - 1x15, 1x12, 1x10, 1x8 reps

3. Seated adductor machine - 1x15, 1x12, 1x10 reps

4. Seated abductor machine - 1x15, 1x12, 1x10 reps

Glutes

1. Table top glute kickbacks – 1x15, 1x15, 1x15 each leg

Calves

1. One legged standing dumbbell calf raises - 1x15, 1x12, 1x10 for each side

2. Seated calf raises - 1x15, 1x12, 1x10 reps

Core

1. Same core as Sunday

Friday

Triceps

1. Close grip bench presses - 1x15, 1x12, 1x10 reps

2. One arm overhead dumbbell triceps extension - 1x15, 1x12 each side

3. One arm dumbbell triceps kickbacks - 1x15, 1x12 each side

Biceps

1. Alternate dumbbell bicep curls - 1x15, 1x12, 10 reps

2. Preacher curls - 1x15, 1x12, 1x10 reps

Cardio

1. Treadmill or elliptical – 25-30 minutes

Week 3: Heavy Week

1. Go up 2.5-10lbs from week 1 on all exercises

2. A 2.5-5 lb increase on smaller muscle groups and a 5-10 lb increase on larger muscle groups

3. Go to failure on the last set

Sunday: Cardio 25-30 minutes + core

Monday: Back + hamstrings

Tuesday: Chest + triceps

Wed: Rest

Thursday: Shoulders + biceps + core

Friday: Quadriceps + calves

Saturday: Rest or light walking

Sunday

Cardio

1. Tread mile or rowing machine – 25-30 minutes

Core

1. Single prone leg lifts - 1x15, 1x15 reps

2. Bicycles - 1x15, 1x15, 1x15reps

3. Side plank reaches - 1x10, 1x10 each side

Monday

Back

1. Barbell back rows - 1x12, 1x10, 1x8 reps

2. Reverse grip pull downs - 1x12, 1x10, 1x8 reps

3. Bar deadlifts - 1x12, 1x10, 1x8 reps

4. Chin ups - 1x12, 1x10, 1x8 reps (use assisted chin up machine if necessary)

Hamstrings

1. Lying leg curls - 1x12, 1x10, 1x8 reps

2. Seated leg curls - 1x12, 1x10, 1x8reps

Tuesday

Chest

1. Flat bench press - 1x12, 1x10, 1x8 reps

2. Incline bench press - 1x12, 1x10, 1x8 reps

3. Incline dumbbell fly - 1x12, 1x10, 1x8 reps

4. Dumbbell pullovers - 1x12, 1x10, 1x8 reps

Triceps

1. Bar skull crushers - 1x12, 1x10, 1x8 reps

2. Pulley push downs - 1x12, 1x10, 1x8 reps

3. Pulley rope triceps overhead extensions - 1x12, 1x10, 1x8 reps

Thursday

Shoulders

1. Dumbbell side laterals - 1x12, 1x10, 1x8 reps

2. Seated barbell front shoulder press - 1x12, 1x10, 1x8, 1x6 reps

3. Bent over dumbbell rear laterals raises- 1x12, 1x10, 1x8 reps

Biceps

1. Seated machine biceps curls - 1x12, 1x10, 1x8 reps

2. Barbell biceps curls - 1x12, 1x10, 1x8 reps

Core

1. Same workout as Sunday

Friday

Quadriceps

1. Back squats - 1x12, 1x10, 1x8 reps

2. Leg press - 1x12, 1x10, 1x8 reps

3. Leg extensions - 1x12, 1x10, 1x8 reps

4. Hack squats - 1x12, 1x10, 1x8 reps

Calves

1. Standing calf raises - 1x12, 1x10, 1x8 reps

2. Seated calf raises - 1x12, 1x10, 1x8 reps

Week 4: Medium - Light week

1. Keep the same weights as week 2

2. We are increasing the resistance by increasing the reps

3. Do not go to failure for any sets

Sunday: Cardio 25-30 minutes + core

Monday: Chest + back

Tuesday: Shoulders + glutes + hamstrings

Wednesday: Rest

Thursday: Quadriceps + calves + core

Friday: Triceps + biceps + cardio

Saturday: Rest

Sunday

Cardio

1. Treadmill or elliptical – 25-30 minutes

Core

1. Bird dogs - 1x15, 1x15 reps

2. Dumbbell side tilts - 1x15, 1x15 each side

3. Stability ball passes - 1x12, 1x12, 1x12 reps

Monday

Back

1. Close grip V-bar pull down - 1x20, 1x15, 1x12 reps

2. Machine back row - 1x20, 1x15, 1x12 reps

3. High pulley pullovers - 1x20, 1x15, 1x12 reps

4. One arm dumbbell rows - 1x20, 1x15, 1x12 reps

Chest

1. Incline dumbbell chest press - 1x20, 1x15, 1x12 reps

2. Regular pushups - 1x20, 1x20, 1x20 reps

3. Cable crossovers - 1x20, 1x15, 1x12 reps

Tuesday

Shoulders

1. Machine shoulder press - 1x20, 1x15, 1x12 reps

2. Pulley face pulls - 1x20, 1x15, 1x12 reps

3. Barbell upright rows - 1x20, 1x15, 1x12 reps

Glutes

1. Table top glute kicks – 1x15, 1x15, 1x15 reps

Hamstrings

1. Dumbbell stiff legged dead lifts - 1x20, 1x15, 1x12 reps

2. Seated hamstring curls - 1x20, 1x15, 1x12 reps

Thursday

Quadriceps

1. Leg extensions - 1x20, 1x15, 1x12, 1x10 reps

2. Seated adductor machine - 1x20, 1x15, 1x12, 1x10 reps

3. Seated abductor machine - 1x20, 1x15, 1x12 reps

4. Plie dumbbell squats - 1x20, 1x15, 1x12, 1x10 reps

Calves

1. Seated calf raises - 1x20, 1x15, 1x12 reps

2. One legged standing dumbbell calf raises - 1x20, 1x15, 1x12 for each side

Core

1. Same workout as Sunday

Friday

Triceps

1. Seated overhead dumbbell triceps extensions - 1x20, 1x15, 1x12 reps

2. Close grip bench presses - 1x20, 1x15, reps

3. One arm dumbbell kickbacks - 1x20, 1x15 reps

Biceps

1. Preacher bar bicep curls - 1x20, 1x15, 1x10 reps

2. Alternate dumbbell biceps curls - 1x20, 1x15, 1x12 reps

Cardio

1. Bike or outside run – 25-30 minutes

Week 5 : Heavy Week

1. Figure out your 1RM

2. Go to up to 90% of your 1RM for all exercises.

3. Go to failure for the last set.

Sunday: Cardio 25-30 minutes + core

Monday: Chest + triceps

Tuesday: Back + biceps

Wednesday: Rest

Thursday: Chest/back (warm up) + Shoulders + core

Friday: Quadriceps + hamstrings + calves

Saturday: Rest or light walking

Sunday

Cardio

1. Elliptical or Rower – 25-30 minutes

Core

1. Hold superman – 1x20, 1x20 seconds

2. Dumbbell crunches – 1x20, 1x20, 1x20 reps

3. Scissor kicks – 1x20, 1x20, 1x20 reps

4. Side planks – 1x25 seconds each side

Monday

Chest

1. Flat dumbbell bench press - 1x10, 1x8,1x6 reps

2. Machine chest fly - 1x10, 1x8, 1x6 reps

3. Incline dumbbell bench press - 1x10, 1x8, 1x6 reps

Triceps

1. Rope triceps push downs - 1x10, 1x8, 1x6 reps

2. Decline dumbbell triceps extensions - 1x10, 1x8reps

3. Mini-dips - 1x12, 1x10 reps

Tuesday

Back

1. Close grip v-bar pull downs - 1x10, 1x8, 1x6 reps

2. Seated v-bar back pulley rows - 1x10, 1x8, 1x6 reps

3. Under grip chin ups - 1x10, 1x8, 1x6 reps (use assisted chin up machine if necessary)

4. One arm dumbbell back rows - 1x10, 1x8, 1x6 reps

Biceps

1. Machine biceps curls - 1x10, 1x8, 1x6 reps

2. Incline dumbbell biceps curls - 1x10, 1x8, 1x6 reps

Thursday

Chest/Back warm up (go lighter)

1. Machine pull down to front – 1x10, 1x8, 1x6 reps

2. Machine bench press – 1x10, 1x8, 1x6 reps

Shoulders

1. Seated dumbbell shoulder presses - 1x10, 1x8, 1x6 reps

2. Cable side laterals - 1x10, 1x8, 1x6 reps

3. Machine rear delt fly - 1x10, 1x8, 1x6 reps

Core

1. Same as Sunday

Friday

Quadriceps

1. Back squats - 1x10, 1x8, 1x6, 1x4 reps

2. Leg extensions - 1x10, 1x8, 1x6, 1x4 reps

3. Machine leg press - 1x10, 1x8, 1x6, 1x4 reps

Hamstrings

1. Standing leg curls - 1x10, 1x8 1x6 reps

2. Lying leg curls - 1x10, 1x8, 1x6 reps

Calves

1. Leg press machine calf pushes - 1x12, 1x10, 1x8 reps

2. Seated calf raises - 1x12, 1x10, 1x8 reps

Week 6: Medium Light Week

1. Go up 2.5-5 lbs for small muscle groups from week 4

2. Go up 5-10 lbs for larger muscle groups from week 4

3. Do not go to failure on any set

Sunday: Cardio 20-25 minutes + core

Monday: Chest + quadriceps

Tuesday: Shoulders + triceps

Wednesday: Rest

Thursday: Back + hamstrings + calves

Friday: Glutes + biceps + core +cardio

Saturday: Rest

Sunday

Cardio

1. Tread mile or bike – 25-30 minutes

Core

1. On stomach back extensions - 1x15, 1x15 reps

2. Cable crunches - 1x15, 1x15, 1x15 reps

3. Reverse crunches - 1x15, 1x15, 1x15 reps

4. Dumbbell side tilts - 1x15, 1x15 each side

Monday

Chest

1. Incline dumbbell flye - 1x15, 1x12, 1x10 reps

2. Flat machine bench press - 1x15, 1x12, 1x10 reps

3. Machine chest flye - 1x15, 1x12, 1x10 reps

Quadriceps

1. Holding dumbbell squats - 1x15, 1x12, 1x10, 1x8 reps

2. Leg extensions - 1x15, 1x12, 1x10, 1x8 reps

3. Side lunges on bosu - 1x15, 1x15, 1x15 for each side

Tuesday

Shoulders

1. Dumbbell front laterals - 1x15, 1x12, 1x10 reps

2. Dumbbell side laterals - 1x15, 1x12, 1x10 reps

3. Dumbbell rear laterals - 1x15, 1x12, 1x10 reps

Triceps

1. W-bar skull crushers - 1x15, 1x12, 1x10 reps

2. Rope pulley overhead triceps extensions - 1x15, 1x12 reps

3. Triceps dip machine - 1x15, 1x12 reps

Thursday

Back

1. T-bar rows - 1x15, 1x12, 1x10 reps

2. Seated back pulley rows - 1x15, 1x12, 1x10 reps

3. Under grip pull downs - 1x15, 1x12, 1x10 reps

Hamstrings

1. Supine one legged ball curls - 1x10, 1x10, 1x10 for each leg

2. Dumbbell stiff legged dead lifts - 1x15, 1x12, 1x10 reps

Calves

1. Seated calf raises - 1x15, 1x12, 1x10 reps

2. Plate loader leg press calf pushes - 1x15, 1x12, 1x10 reps

Friday

Glutes

1. Standing one legged pulley glute kicks – 1x15, 1x12, 1x10 each side

Biceps

1. Bar pulley biceps curls - 1x15, 1x12, 1x10 reps

2. Pulley overhead cable curls - 1x15, 1x12, 1x10 reps

Core

1. Same as Sunday workout

Cardio

1. Treadmill or bike – 25-20 minutes

Week 7: Heavy Week

1. Go up 2.5- 5lbs for smaller muscle groups from week 5

2. Go up 5-10 lbs for larger muscle groups from week 5

3. Go to failure for the last set

Sunday: Cardio + core

Monday: Chest + triceps

Tuesday: Back + biceps

Wednesday: Rest

Thursday: Chest/back (warm up) + shoulders + core

Friday: Quadriceps + hamstrings + calves

Saturday: Rest

Sunday

Cardio

1. Rower or Tread mile – 25-30 minutes

Core

1. Single prone leg lifts - 1x15, 1x15 each leg

2. Elbow plank – 30 seconds x 2

3. V-sit holds – 30 seconds x 2

4. Standing medicine ball twists - 1 minute x1

Monday

Chest

1. Incline dumbbell chest press - 1x12, 1x10, 1x8 reps

2. Machine chest fly - 1x12, 1x10, 1x8 reps

3. Flat dumbbell bench press - 1x12, 1x10, 1x8 reps

Triceps

1. Rope triceps push downs - 1x12, 1x10, 1x8 reps

2. Partial mini- dips - 1x12, 1x10 reps

3. Decline dumbbell triceps extensions - 1x12, 1x10 reps

Tuesday

Back

1. Close grip V-bar pull down - 1x12, 1x10, 1x8 reps

2. One arm back dumbbell rows - 1x12, 1x10, 1x8 reps

3. Under grip chin ups - 1x12, 1x10, 1x8 reps (use machine assisted chin ups if needed)

4. Seated V-bar back pulley rows - 1x12, 1x10, 1x8 reps

Biceps

1. Incline dumbbell curls - 1x12, 1x10, 1x8 reps

2. Machine biceps curls - 1x12, 1x10, 1x8 reps

Thursday

Chest/back (warm up)

1. Lat pull down to front – 1x12, 1x10, 1x8 reps

2. Machine bench press – 1x12, 1x10, 1x8 reps

Shoulders

1. Cable side laterals - 1x12, 1x10, 1x8 reps

2. Dumbbell shoulder presses - 1x12, 1x10, 1x8 reps

3. Machine rear delt fly - 1x12, 1x10, 1x8 reps

Core

1. Same workout as Sunday

Friday

Quadriceps

1. Machine leg press - 1x12, 1x10, 1x8, 1x6 reps

2. Leg extensions - 1x12, 1x10, 1x8, 1x6 reps

3. Back squats - 1x12, 1x10, 1x8, 1x6 reps

Hamstrings

1. Lying leg curls - 1x12, 1x10, 1x8 reps

2. Standing leg curls - 1x12, 1x10, 1x8 reps

Calves

1. Seated calf raises - 1x12, 1x10, 1x8 reps

2. Leg press calf pushes - 1x12, 1x10, 1x8 reps

Week 8: Light Medium Week

1. Use same weights as week 6 and we will increase resistance by reps

2. Do not go to failure any set

Sunday: Cardio + core

Monday: Chest + quadriceps

Tuesday: Shoulders + triceps

Wednesday: Rest

Thursday: Back + hamstrings + calves

Friday: Glutes + biceps + core + cardio

Saturday: Rest

Sunday

Cardio

1. Bike or tread mile – 25-30 minutes

Core

1. Land swimming – 1x20, 1x20 seconds

2. Stability ball pikes – 1x15, 1x15, 1x15 reps

3. Standing oblique bar twists - 1x1 minute

Monday

Chest

1. Flat machine bench press - 1x20, 1x15, 1x12 reps

2. Incline dumbbell fly - 1x20, 1x15, 1x12 reps

3. Machine chest fly- 1x20, 1x15, 1x12 reps

Quadriceps

1. Leg extensions - 1x20, 1x15, 1x12, 1x10 reps

2. Holding dumbbell squats - 1x20, 1x15, 1x12 reps

3. Side lunges on bosu - 1x15, 1x15, 1x15 for each side

Tuesday

Shoulders

1. Side laterals - 1x20, 1x15, 1x12 reps

2. Front laterals - 1x20, 1x15, 1x12 reps

3. Rear laterals - 1x20, 1x15, 1x12 reps

Triceps

1. Triceps dip machine - 1x20, 1x15, 1x12 reps

2. Rope overhead triceps extensions - 1x20, 1x15 reps

3. W-bar skull crushers - 1x20, 1x15 reps

Thursday

Back

1. Under grip pull downs - 1x20, 1x15, 1x12 reps

2. Pull down to front - 1x20, 1x15, 1x12 reps

3. T-bar rows - 1x20, 1x15, 1x12 reps

4. Seated back pulley rows - 1x20, 1x15, 1x12 reps

Hamstrings

1. Dumbbell deadlifts - 1x20, 1x15, 1x12 reps

2. Supine hamstring ball curls - 1x15, 1x15, 1x15 reps

Calves

1. Plate loader calf pushes - 1x20, 1x15, 1x12 reps

2. Seated calf raises - 1x20, 1x15, 1x12 reps

Friday

Glutes

1. Standing one legged pulley glute kicks – 1x20, 1x15, 1x10 each side

Biceps

1. Overhead cable curls - 1x20, 1x15, 1x10 reps

2. Bar pulley curls - 1x20, 1x15, 1x10 reps

Core

1. Same workout as Sunday

Cardio

1. Bike or elliptical – 25-30 minutes

CONCLUSION

Train, grunt, eat, rest and grow. In order to have muscular growth you must follow the previous sentence, but not necessarily the grunting.

Building muscle on your body is like creating a new outside shell. It becomes your new armor and skin. This new armor helps to build confidence and not to mention how good it makes you feel.

Once you have built the ultimate physique, there is a great sense accomplishment in your everyday life.

I hope you have learned more about what it takes to build some serious muscle mass. All that eating, sleeping, supplements, and hours in the gym.

It takes hard work, but in the end, the results speak for themselves.

ABOUT THE AUTHOR

Paul Nam has been in the fitness industry and a personal trainer for over 20 years. He started bodybuilding at the age of 18 and became the Junior Mackenzie Bodybuilding Champion at 19. He has since then competed in over 25 bodybuilding, fitness, and martial arts competitions. He has trained in Olympic style boxing, Brazilian jui-jitsu, muay thai, wrestling, and holds a red belt in tae kwon do.

Paul owns a fitness studio in Toronto, builds mobile training apps, and is now writing a series of books. He also owns an online training company and is focusing on bringing a few new inventions to the world.

CERTIFICATIONS:

Can-Fit Pro -Personal Training Specialist

YMCA - Fitness Instructor

Children's Fitness Coach

Fascia – Movement & Assessments

Yoga - Level 1

Pilates Mat - Level 1

Fitness Kickboxing - Level 1

MMA – Level 1

CPR & First Aid

Nutritionist

Sports Consultant

Made in the USA
Columbia, SC
15 December 2020

28320341R00052